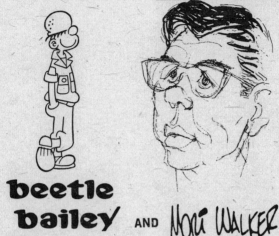

beetle bailey AND *Mort Walker*

Here we see the two people most responsible for the success of **Beetle Bailey**—Beetle himself and his famous creator, Mort Walker, as caricatured by fellow artist Emory Clark. Walker's artful genius and wry humor have catapulted his reluctant army private to international stardom and popularity. One of the most successful comic strips in the history of comics, **Beetle Bailey** is syndicated in nearly 1,100 newspapers and enjoyed by more than 50 million readers in the U.S. and 43 other countries. It has also won every major prize awarded by the comics profession.

Artist Walker sees Beetle and his buddies as a "U.S. Army made up primarily of civilians. Beetle is typical of these civilians who never become real soldiers. He resists this unnatural way of life in every way he can."

beetle bailey ®

by MORT WALKER

tempo books

GROSSET & DUNLAP, INC.
Publishers   New York

SOME OF THE GANG AT CAMP SWAMPY

KILLER
DILLER

SGT. ORVILLE
SNORKEL

ZERO

LT. SONNY
FUZZ

COOKIE

PLATO

CAPT. SAM
SCABBARD

GEN. AMOS. T.
HALFTRACK

CHAPLAIN
STANEGLASS

3-2

TRY TO PICK OUT YOUR OPPONENT'S WEAK SPOT AND KEEP HAMMERING AWAY AT IT

CAMP SWAMPY

HERE, I'LL DEMONSTRATE ON A VOLUNTEER. BEETLE, STAND UP

4-25

GEE, I HARDLY KNOW WHERE TO BEGIN

MORT WALKER

3-31

WHEN'S HIS FURLOUGH GOING TO BE OVER, SIR?

MORT WALKER

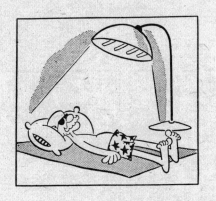

WE DON'T TAKE ANY CHANCES SINCE HE GOT BURNED LAST MONTH

2-23

6-16

SARGE, DON'T WALK BESIDE ME! SOLDIERS AREN'T ALLOWED TO FRATERNIZE WITH OFFICERS!

BUT I'M GOING TO THE PX, TOO!

2-20

LOOK! I DON'T CARE **WHAT** YOU DO JUST AS LONG AS YOU STAY BEHIND ME!!

YES, SIR

HUP, TWO, THREE, FOUR...

MORT WALKER

BUNNY, WHY DOES YOUR FATHER ALWAYS LOOK AT ME AND WALK AWAY SHAKING HIS HEAD?

OH, ER-- HE HAS SOMETHING BOTHERING HIM

IN HIS NECK?

ON THE COUCH!!!

MORT WALKER

12-19

I **LIKE** THIS SUGGESTION-BOX IDEA

SUGGESTI

BEETLE, MY PANTS ARE READY AT THE CLEANERS

SO WHAT?

2-15

GO GET MY PANTS!

I THOUGHT THEY DELIVERED!

ONLY FOR OFFICERS!

SERGEANTS HAVE TO GET THEIR **OWN** STUFF!

OH...

MORT WALKER

I'LL BET BEETLE JUST SNEAKED OFF! I FELT THAT COLD CHILL ON MY NECK AGAIN!

6-18

CALL FOR THE CHOPPERS

BUT, SIR, THEY DROPPED EVERYTHING WE ORDERED FOR DINNER... CORN, ROAST BEEF, APPLE PIE.....

I THAID, **CALL FOR THE CHOPPERS!**

OH

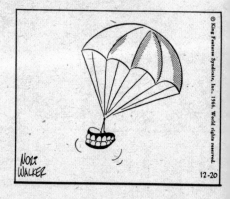

NOG WALKER

12-20

6-15

MORT
WALKER